The Ultimate Feng Shui Guide to a Happier Life

How to Improve Every Aspect of Your Life with Feng Shui

Kate Dunn

This book is dedicated to anyone looking to empower every aspect of their life with Feng Shui. Whether you need help in relationships, finances, health or love Feng Shui is easy to implement and works.

Copyright Act of 1976, the scanning, uploading and electronic sharing of any part of this book without the explicit written consent or permission of the publisher constitutes unlawful piracy and the theft of intellectual property.

If you would like to use material or content from this book (other than for review purposes), prior written permission must be obtained from the publisher.

You can contact the publishing company at admin@speedypublishing.com. Thank you for not infringing on the author's rights.

Speedy Publishing LLC (c) 2014
40 E. Main St., #1156
Newark, DE 19711
www.speedypublishing.co

Ordering Information:
Quantity sales; Special discounts are available on quantity purchases by corporations, associations, and others. For details, contact the "Special Sales Department" at the address above.

This is a reprint book.

Manufactured in the United States of America

Table of Contents

Publisher's Notes i

Chapter 1: About Feng Shui 1

Chapter 2: Qi Energy and Feng Shui 5

Chapter 3: Feng Shui and Yin/Yang 10

Chapter 4: The 5 Elements in Feng Shui 13

Chapter 5: The Feng Shui Kua Number 26

Chapter 6: Defining Your "Ba Gua" 30

Chapter 7: Finding the Missing Ba Gua Areas in Your Residence 39

Chapter 8: How to Utilize Ba Gua Areas 46

Chapter 9: The Art of Feng Shui 62

Meet the Author 65

Publisher's Notes

Disclaimer

This publication is intended to provide helpful and informative material. It is not intended to diagnose, treat, cure, or prevent any health problem or condition, nor is intended to replace the advice of a physician. No action should be taken solely on the contents of this book. Always consult your physician or qualified health-care professional on any matters regarding your health and before adopting any suggestions in this book or drawing inferences from it.

The author and publisher specifically disclaim all responsibility for any liability, loss or risk, personal or otherwise, which is incurred as a consequence, directly or indirectly, from the use or application of any contents of this book.

Any and all product names referenced within this book are the trademarks of their respective owners. None of these owners have sponsored, authorized, endorsed, or approved this book.

Always read all information provided by the manufacturers' product labels before using their products. The author and publisher are not responsible for claims made by manufacturers.

Chapter 1: About Feng Shui

Today we find many people reaching outside of the natural born cultures and belief systems to help them in their lives. You find people searching for spiritual ways to improve their lives so they gravitate towards things other cultures use to improve theirs with. Feng Shui is one such practice that many people are using today to enhance their living spaces and lives.

Feng Shui once called Fung Shoo ee is a very ancient science deriving from China. Feng Shui is a system of what is referred to as Chinese Aesthetics. Its philosophy is premised on the ideas of the "laws" of heaven (astronomy) and Earth (geography) should be utilized to improve one's life for the better. The concept behind Feng Shui is if you live in harmony with these laws you will have positive results in your own life.

If you translate the words Feng Shui into English it literally means wind-water. Feng Shui incorporates elements from nature in its practice. It is a very accurate practice which utilizes a compass called "luo pan" to pinpoint specific directions to make one's life better. The compass gives the Feng Shui practitioner specific directions/locations to find the auspicious direction to utilize. Until the magnetic compass was created Feng Shui relied on astronomy to pinpoint the relation between man and this universe.

A Little History

Facts are what we look at though out history to give us validity of a practice or belief. It is done by proving the fact or facts concrete existence in a given society. A society that uses something today that dates back to prehistoric times obviously found merit in its practices. Indications are that Feng Shui goes way back to prehistoric man.

Beginning with cities in Erlitou China dating as far as 1500 BC to 2000 BC; the ruins show that the early inhabitants followed rules of Feng Shui by the arrangement and placement of their graves and tombs. History points to the traces of Feng Shui being used in Ancient Chinese provinces dating 3000 BC. Devices and formulas resembling the modern ones used today in Feng Shui were found on jade artifacts.

Evidence of Ancient Feng Shui is indicated by the doors of the Bangpo archeological site in China dating back to 4000 BC. It was a well-organized Neolithic settlement. The fact that it was so well organized and the dwellings were aligned with a pattern of stars called Yingshi right after the winter solstice indicates that these ancient people utilized Feng Shui. By placing their homes in the direction of these stars they were increasing the heat, warmth, and light in their spaces via solar radiation. Later in the Zhou dynasty the same star consolations were utilized to determine the best time to build a capital city.

A grave site in Puyang dating back to 4000 BC is really a constellation map of the Tiger and Dragon as well as the big Dipper called Beidou which is on the compass today. It is located on a north-south access. (In Feng Shui the directions correlate to specific heavenly aspects.)

The earliest devices found in ancient Chinese Feng Shui all predate the magnetic compass. Of the earliest devices found is the "gnomon" which is the part of a sundial that casts a shadow. The Chinese used circumpolar stars to pinpoint the North-South directions of their settlements. Then they further bisected the angle between the four directions of the rising and setting of the sun to find the North. Rituals were utilized by a diviner to use this instrument to keep abreast of current happenings in the sky. This was done to set and reset the device according to the occurrences.

We see the oldest examples of Feng Shui instruments which are the astrolabes called Luiren or Shi. These instruments were historically used by what we refer to as the classical astronomers, navigators and astrologers. What this device did was locate and predict the positions of the Sun, Moon, Planets and Stars by determining the local times based on the local latitude as well as surveying and triangulation. Triangulation is the process of locating a point by measuring angles to that point via a base line as opposed to measuring the angle to the point directly thus creating three points that look like a triangle. The Shi looked like a lacquered two sided board with astronomical site lines on it. The earliest found device like this dates back to between 278 and 290 BC. What is interesting is that the markings on this early device and the first magnetic compasses are identical.

The magnetic compass was invented for the practice of Feng Shui. It has been used until today since its invention by those that practice Feng Shui. Traditional Feng Shui instruments include the Luopan or Chinese magnetic compass. The Luopan is a model of the cosmos based on the tortoise shell lines that are used in Chinese divination. At the most basic level it is used to give proper positions of time and space which are all used in Feng Shui. The "**zhinan zhen**" *or* south pointing needle which is the predecessor of the Luopan was the original pointing compass. It was made of two cords and a diagram of four hooks, direction markers and a magnetized spoon in the center.

It is safe to say that Feng Shui must have some merit if it survived since prehistoric times.

Chapter 2: Qi Energy and Feng Shui

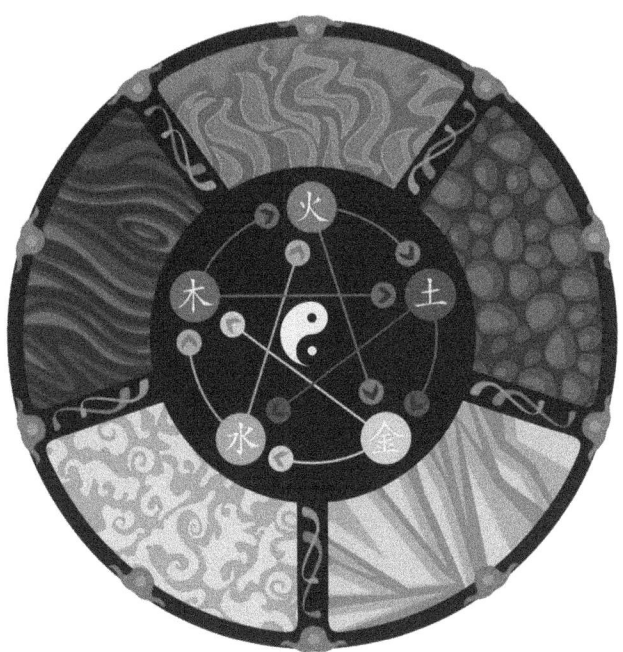

Feng Shui bases it foundation on Taoism and its concept of nature. Taoism believes that all land is alive and filled with Qi. Qi is universal energy which permeates everything. It is the life force in our bodies as well as the energy around buildings and landscape.

Just as we need to keep Qi flowing in our bodies for optimum health; the same applies to Qi in our living environments. The idea is, if you can properly channel the Qi in your living environment so as to create good flow it nourishes the soul. When this happens it will support the flow of good Qi within our bodies. The result is that we will be externally and internally in harmony with our environment and our bodies which is positive. Positivity comes because we are in harmony with both. It is believed that when we are in balance and positive; our lives reflect that energy and we receive positivity back to us as a result. In Feng Shui positive Qi or Sheng Qi is created when we are around or produce things of beauty. This includes internal as well as external beauty. Negative Qi occurs from clutter, ugliness and things done poorly. Negative Qi is produced both externally and internally based on those factors as well.

Sheng is defined as upward moving energy. Sheng Qi uplifts and brightens our lives in a positive swing. Negative Qi or Sha Qi also called Si Qi does the opposite. This negative Qi is referred to as killing or attacking energy. Sha Qi is sharp attacking energy like a point. An example of Sha Qi would be something like a sharp wall pointing at your bed called a poison arrow. In this case the walls sharpness always directed towards you in your bed is an attacking energy directed at your body. An objects proximity to what is causing Sha Qi also determines its severity. So distance is an important factor when determining Sha Qi and how severe it is. The further the object of attack or Sha Qi is away from your personal being and your environment the less of a danger it presents.

Si Qi another negative form of Qi. This type of Qui is a slow decaying energy that leaves you feeling like you are dying or lifeless. This type of negative energy can make one depressed and ill. This is especially true if one is exposed to it for long periods of time. You find this kind of Qi in locations where things like murders, massacres or other tragic events occurred. These types of sites have what is explained as geopathic stresses in Feng Shui.

Qi is manifested also in the theory of Yin and Yang. The Yin and Yang theory is founded on the idea that everything in this universe has a polar opposite. The Yin and Yang theory also states that two opposing forces are interconnected. This concept is illustrated by the Taoist symbol of the Yin and Yang. A circle encompasses two identical symbols in it. One half of the circle contains the black or

Yin side of the circle and the other the Yang or white side. Both symbols within themselves have a circle of the opposite color within them. So the light has a touch of the dark and the dark has a touch of the light and they are both housed within the same circle. It further symbolizes without dark you cannot have light.

Yin is a manifestation of feminine energy and Yang is the masculine manifestation. The Taoist Yin and Yang symbol represents everything in constant motion in the universe. But it also represents how everything is interconnected in the universe; as both the Yin and Yang symbols are within one circle. This illustrates the idea that neither can exist without the other.

Qi as an energy is organized into 5 elements. These 5 elements are based on the major elements in nature. They are Metal, Fire, Water and Earth. Even though these are physical representations Qi is a manifestation of the flow energy and not stagnant or still. Each element is defined as a frequency that also has a wavelength that is unique to that element. These frequencies are visual by specific colors and audible by specific sounds. So, when we look at something, the color it has and the sound it emanates tells us the type of Qi it has or creates.

According to the theory of Qi we exist as 5 elements before we are born. When your parents have sex to create you; the love they have gives off a frequency. Their frequency in unity is similar to yours so it attracts your spirit to them and induces your five elements to come together. Because it is out of love that you are created the first element called is fire which is the heart element and a red light wavelength. Now you have a heartbeat. Next is the will to survive so now comes the metal element or lungs which is white light. With this white wavelength breath occurs. Then the growing fetus begins to take in nourishment from the earth. This is yellow colored. The forth element that comes into being next is the liver because of food intake. It creates enzymes from fruits and vegetables which is the wood element and green light wavelength. This color purifies our systems. Last comes the kidneys which removes wastes and is the water element represented by the black wavelength of light. As a complete being comes into fruition the five vital organs are in balance. Our circulation is optimum along the meridians as a result we emanate a pinkish white aura as we come to life.

The 5 elements are also associated with 8 directions of the earth. Metal is associated with the East and Northwest, Earth with the Southwest and Northeast, Wood with the East and Southeast, Water with the North and last Fire with the South. In Qi terms our bodies Qi also follows the elements and their directions. At our times of birth, the planets create a specific energy in relation to our time of birth and that energy affects us in our lives. This means our birthdays have certain characteristics that affect our Qi flow. In Feng Shui how we are orientated to the earth's energy is one of the main factors in determining the flow of our own Qi and state of being. Our bodily Qi flow is affected by our environmental location.

For example let's use a person and call her Donna. Let's say Donna was born in 1937. There are specific charts relevant to calculating the element and energy flow in Feng Shui Qi. The energy for a female born that year is called Quan (chu wen) or metal element that flows in a Northwestern direction. Her energy field belongs to the Western direction patterns of NW, W, SW and East. So for her energy flow to be at a positive ebb she needs to face her home on one of the Western Directions with its axis W/E or SW/NE.

Also, because of her pattern of directions if she faces in that direction physically; then her body's Qi will flow optimally as well.

On a Psychic level if nothing obstructs Donna's directions she should receive the positive benefits of good Qi. This is because she would ultimately be in alignment with her right directions and the energies that are positive for her. On the other hand, if something blocks the flow of her Qi patterns she will have less Qi flow.

Blockages can be a result of inharmonious directions impeding the flow of Qi. Blocked Qi can force her to face in an inharmonious direction because of the blockage. Due to this she is then placing herself in negative alignment and opening herself to negative energy.

Sometimes we can't avoid the negative directions we turn to but there are things we can do to offset them. Some of the more common Feng Shui "cures" involve simple things like using mirrors to deflect the negative Qi and direct it somewhere else.

The main thing is you want to promote what is called the Cycle of production as much as possible. This means maximizing the opportunities your environment affords. By doing so you allow harmonious elements to nurture each other and remedy those that are inharmonious to a more advantageous possibility. When everything is in harmonious alignment it creates a portal for positive Qi to flow through both within and around one's body.

Chapter 3: Feng Shui and Yin/Yang

The idea of Yin and Yang are very important in the practice of Feng Shui as I pointed out in the previous chapter. Let us review the idea of Yin and Yang again but in more detail. The Yin and Yang symbol represents the balance of harmony between two opposing energies that actually rely on each other to maintain balance. That's why they are two parts of one circle. The universe depends on these two opposing forces that are interconnected. The Yin is considered feminine energy while Yang is masculine.

The feminine energy is represented by the color black but to show its connection to Yang there is a white circle within the black of Yin. And, to show its connection to Yin the Yang color is white but has a little black circle in it. Both Yin and Yang are housed within one larger circle representing the universe.

The Yin energy is considered a passive energy. It is a feminine and receptive energy. As its color is black it represents silence, deep darkness and both slow and relaxed movements. This is the type of energy at night when we sleep. It is also the energy used to replenish ourselves when we are worn out and need to rest or relax.

Yang energy is an active energy. It is a masculine pushing energy. Although the Yang color is white in the symbol of Yin and Yang; Yang is characterized by strong vibrant colors and sounds. It is a light and upward moving energy. It is the type of energy that we use during the day when we are busy and productive.

The color white in Feng Shui which represents the element Metal is also considered the color of purity, innocence and tranquility. It also represents completion, ultimate lessons life gives us and complete wisdom. Being a Metal Element color it also represents beginnings as well as definite endings. It is a crisp, clear, clean and fresh energy.

In Feng Shui terms it is recommended to use white in areas of your home where Metal is the dominant element. This is the West and Northwest directions in your home. White is also a good color to use with bright colors. You do not want white as a dominating color in the East or South East directions of your home. This creates inharmonious energy. In this areas white can be used as an accent to other colors. If you have an all-white room like a meditation room or bathroom it can spread healing vibrations throughout your home if it is in the right direction conducive to the color white.

Black is a color of mystery and sophistication in Feng Shui. It is a color that holds power and protection. In addition to being the color of the night it is also the color of deep waters and the universal void. It's element is Water. The direction for this color and element is North. In Feng Shui this color brings grounding and stability. It is recommended that black be used sparingly indoors and not much higher than eye level. This is because if it is used in large amounts it brings on a heavy feeling. If used in moderation it does bring strength and presence to a room.

Black can be used freely in areas facing North which is Water's direction as well as in the East and South East Which are Woods directions. This is because Water and Wood nurture each other. Black should be avoided in Southern or Fire directions as well as children's rooms, main entries, kitchens and dining rooms. Because Black is a Water element; it can be a good cure for attracting career opportunities if used in the North direction of your home or where you conduct business. Mirrors are also good for Water Element energy and can be used that way if put in a black frame and set in a Northern direction.

CHAPTER 4: THE 5 ELEMENTS IN FENG SHUI

The practice of Feng Shui is heavily rooted in the idea of the 5 elements. It is believed that in the universal scheme of things 5 basic elements in nature dictate the positive and negative energy in the world. All of the Chinese spiritual sciences from astrology to martial arts to Taoism utilize the idea of the 5 elements. The five elements which are Wood, Fire, Metal, Earth and Water all have colors and directions which are used in Feng Shui. The 5 elements also affect our time day and year of birth; with their directions and color. The 5 elements affect our Qi either positively or negatively.

As far as Feng Shui goes it is important to understand the elements and their productive and negative cycles. The elements have cycles that are mutually productive between them or mutually destructive between them. When the elements support each other, then the cycle is considered productive or positive. This means Qi is flowing freely because there is a harmonious relationship between the elements and their corresponding directions. It means that the placement of things around one is in harmony thus Qi is productive and positive. Likewise when elements do not mutually support each other because their energy clashes then it is considered a mutually destructive cycle. This type of destructive cycle means that the flow of Qi is blocked and there is inharmonious energy being produced that does the blocking. The things around one are in conflict with the directions and elements so there is destructive energy prevailing.

In the Productive Cycle:

- Fire nurtures Earth
- Earth nurtures Metal
- Metal nurtures Water
- Water nurtures Wood
- Wood nurtures Fire.

In the Destructive Cycle:

- Wood destroys Earth
- Earth destroys Water
- Water destroys Fire
- Fire destroys Metal
- Metal destroys Wood.

The way an element reacts with another is based on its harmonic interactive factor with that element. Their relationship to each other either creates positive or negative energy. Two nurturing elements are harmonious and create positive energy. At the same time two elements that are destructive to each other cause negative energy.

By understanding this principle you can bring harmony into a living space by either creative productive Qi in the space by using the elements that are harmonious to each other. You can also remedy the destructive energy created by removing the destructive elements and placing the ones in harmony in the right spots. Also based on this idea is if you know your astrological element then you can also utilize that in the home to further create a harmonious environment for your own flow of energy.

All of Feng Shui utilizes the 5 elements in application. The 5 elements balance energy in a space much like the principles of Yin and Yang when used harmoniously. The eight directions which we will talk about in the chapter on Ba Gua also use the elements.

Each Element has one two or three colors as well as a direction that it governs. Here is a chart that breaks this down for you.

Element	Energy Type	Color	Direction
Fire	Yang Energy (Energizing)	Red	South
Earth	Neutral Energy (Grounding and Supporting Energy)	Yellow	Center (Dominant) (also South West and Northwest)
Water	Yin Energy	Black	North
Metal	Yin and Yang	White or Gold	West
Wood	Yin and Yang	Green	East

The Affinities of the Elements

Elements are in affinity in Feng Shui when the work together and create positive Qi. This is the Elements that are in affinity with each other:

- Water helps Wood (water helps plants and trees to grow)
- Wood helps Fire (Wood helps fire to Burn)
- Fire produces Dust (Earth)
- Earth helps Mineral (Metal) to form
- Metal can hold Water

You can see how in nature they nurture one another and there is a positive natural connection between the two elements.

These ideas give way to:

- Water is Woods supporting element;
- Wood releases the power of Water

- Wood is the supporting element of Fire
- Fire releases the power of Wood

- Fire is the supporting element for Earth
- Earth releases the power of Fire

- Earth is the supporting element of Metal
- Metal releases the power of Earth

- Metal is the supporting element of Water
- Water releases the power of Metal

Each element that is in affinity with each other enhances the attribute that that element has. Elements that are destructive or oppose each other do not support each other or enhance their attributes. They are in conflict with each other and destroy the positive aspects each has.

Elements that oppose each other or are destructive to each other:

- Water extinguishes Fire but,
- Fire can evaporate Water.

- Wood breaks the ground (Earth) but,
- Earth can bury Wood.

- Fire melts Metal but,
- Metal is not melted until Fire is extinguished.

- Earth absorbs Water but,
- Water can over flow the Earth.

- Metal cuts Wood but,
- Wood can make Metal dull before the Wood is cut.

With these ideas in mind we can say:

- Water and Fire are enemies
- Water overwhelms the movement of Fire

- Wood and Earth are enemies
- Wood overwhelms the movement of Earth

- Fire and Metal are enemies
- Fire overwhelms the movement of Metal

- Earth and Water are enemies
- Earth overwhelms the movement of Water

- Metal and Wood are enemies
- Metal overwhelms the movement of Wood

We can see that these elements do not work in harmony with each other. They actually can destroy each other's positive attributes. So when using Feng Shui you do not put two elements that are inharmonious together. If you do then you are creating negative energy by the sheer fact of their relationship to one another.

The Characteristics of the Elements

Each element has specific characteristics to it. The characteristics include the direction it governs its color and what it does as an element.

Fire - is a forceful energy. The colors that represent this element range from oranges to reds to pinks to purples. Bright colors that also bounce and energize lights belong to the fire element. The fire colors represent expansion and transformation. The shapes associated with the element of fire are angular like pyramids, triangles, diamonds and sunbursts. These shapes send energy at a fast speed in all directions and also because of this create movement and change. It is the fire element that gives you high energy in anything you do. This includes career, leisure activities and with couples sex. The direction of fire is south.

Earth - is a grounding and supportive energy. The colors of this element range from Yellows to Beige /Brown Earth tones. Muted tones also may fall into the earth element. These are colors of slowing down energy. The shapes associated with the earth element are rectangles and squares. These are considered grounding horizontal shapes. Changing artwork and windows from portrait to landscape can help increase earth energy in a home. The earth element in the home adds stability and a feeling of security. It helps make each family member feel nurtured. The direction of Earth is either center dominant on the BaGua map (which I will talk about later) or South West or North West.

Wood - is personal growth energy. The colors associated with wood are greens for growth (touches of purple are sometimes added in the wood area for living with abundance.) Wood encompasses colors that are clear and energizing. This element represents vertical moving energy and is associated with things shaped like cylinders and columns. Wood brings oxygen to the home. It is used in health cures in relation to living environments. Prosperity is also governed by wood. Its direction is east.

Water- is the element of release and renewal. The colors of this element range from dark blues to black. The colors of the element water encourage wisdom. The energy of water is represented by any shape that is flowing. Still water is represented by any shape that holds water containing it like a womb. Moving water are shapes that are cascading or rippling. The energy of water flows to the sides and then down. Water is an element that refreshes. When it flows freely it represents abundance. When you use the water element in your home you purify, refresh and add abundance of energy to it. The direction for Water is north.

Metal - is the mental power element. The colors of metal are white, silver, grey and sometimes gold. The colors of the rainbow are also colors of this element and are associated with healing and creativity. The colors of metal are shape and represent intelligence. The shape representing metal is the circle. The energy in a circle is constantly moving in an expanding cycle sending energy outward. Metal is viewed by many as being cold and unfeeling but when used correctly it is actually stimulating to create efficiency and clarity of mind as well as purpose. This element actually helps with such things like well-defined goals and good qualities in the home. If everyone is on the same page in a living or working environment there is like purpose in accomplishing the same goals and metal helps set the tone for this. Metals direction is west.

Every Element has a Yin or Yang quality and there are times when they can have both. For example, Yin Metal would be soft silver that bends while Yang metal is hard steel. Plants that are green and healthy are considered Yang while dead and woody plants are considered Yin. Paintings of water and wavy curtains are Yin. Water energy with fountains and aquariums are Yang. Fire is Yang. But, as I previously stated there are times when an element can have both qualities. For example soft glowing candles are yin as are cinnamon incense. There are many examples of Yin fire element.

In terms of Feng Shui, when you understand the concept of harmonious and inharmonious aspects of elements, you can incorporate them into your home. For example if you were born under a fire element year you would not have too much water element objects or colors in your home. This is because Water destroys fire. In this case you would not use too much black or dark blues, waterfalls, aquariums, ponds and things of that nature in or around your home. You would however incorporate a lot of wood elements in your home because Wood nurtures fire. You would also try and sleep in a room facing south or in the south end of your home or apartment because that is Fire's direction.

Here is a chart to find your Element and Direction based on the hour of your birth.

Time	Element	Direction
11pm to 1 am	Wood	Face North
1am to 3 am	Wood	Face North and North East
3am to 5am	Fire	Face East to East North
5am to 7am	Fire	Face East
7am to 9am	Earth	Face East To South East
9am to 11am	Earth	Face South to South East
11am to 1pm	Metal	Face South
1pm to 3pm	Metal	Face South to South East
3pm to 5pm	Water	Face West to South West
5pm to 7pm	Water	Face West

| 7pm to 9pm | Water | Face West to North West |
| 9pm to 11pm | Water | North to North West |

A Chart to Check your Element against the Year of Your Birth

Year of the Rat	1900 Metal, 1912 Water, 1924 Wood, 1936 Fire, 1948 Earth, 1960 Metal, 1972 Water, 1984 Wood, 1996 Fire
Year of the Ox	1901 Metal, 1913 Water, 1925 Wood, 1937 Fire, 1949 Earth, 1961 Metal, 1973 Water, 1985 Wood, 1997 Fire
Year of the Tiger	1902 Water, 1914 Wood, 1926 Fire, 1938 Earth, 1950 Metal, 1962 Water, 1974 Wood, 1986 Fire, 1998 Earth
Year of the Rabbit	1903 Water; 1915 Wood; 1927 Fire; 1939 Earth; 1951 Metal; 1963 Water; 1975 Wood; 1987 Fire; 1999 Earth
Year of the Dragon	1904 Wood; 1916 Fire; 1928 Earth; 1940 Metal; 1952 Water; 1964 Wood; 1976 Fire; 1988 Earth; 2000 Metal
Year of the Snake	1905 Wood; 1917 Fire; 1929 Earth; 1941 Metal; 1953 Water; 1965 Wood; 1977 Fire; 1989 Earth; 2001 Metal
Year of the Horse	1906 Fire; 1918 Earth; 1930 Metal; 1942 Water; 1954 Wood; 1966 Fire; 1978 Earth; 1990 Metal; 2002 Water

Year of the Monkey	1907 Fire; 1919 Earth; 1931 Metal; 1943 Water; 1955 Wood; 1967 Fire; 1979 Earth; 1991 Metal; 2003 Water
Year of the Rooster	1908 Earth; 1921 Metal; 1933 Water; 1945 Wood; 1957 Fire; 1969 Earth; 1981 Metal; 1993 Water; 2005 Wood
Year of the Dog	1909 Metal; 1922 Water; 1934 Wood; 1946 Fire; 1958 Earth; 1970 Metal; 1982 Water; 1994 Wood; 2006 Fire
Year of the Boar	1910 Metal; 1923 Water; 1935 Wood; 1947 Fire; 1959 Earth; 1971 Metal; 1983 Water; 1995 Wood; 2007 Fire

In Feng Shui when we use the elements properly they create a positive flow of Qi in our living environment and in turn enhance our Qi internally. For instance a Fire element person would Place red objects in the auspicious direction will bring Yang energy to that area. If space is limited and needs Yang energy you can always place a red or orange candle in that area as well.

Earth energy is nurturing and warming. It is soothing as well as improves marital and close relationships if objects and colors pertaining to the element are utilized in the southwest direction. It also stimulates learning in this direction. Since Earth nurtures Metal, metallic areas also benefit from earthen objects. To enhance knowledge and education you can put things like terra cotta pots, crystals and ceramics in northeastern directions in a meta-elemental area.

Metal is in general a positive Yang element. If you have an area in your home that has too much Yin you can place a metal shiny hard object to increase the Yang energy flow in that area. The rule of thumb is things that are soft in nature a Yang and those that are hard are Yin. You can also harmonize the blending of Yin and Yang energies together by using Chimes in water areas, where the water energy needs to flow.

Water is also the element of prosperity and wealth. If water features are added to Northern areas which are the direction for career then it can help with career aspirations. A water element object placed in a wealth area or direction is very auspicious. You do not want to however place a water object in the bedroom. Also areas where water has stagnancy like the bathroom. It is not recommended to over stimulate this area with Water elements since money is represented by Water and in this case Water is always going down the drain and being flushed in the bathroom. It is also wise for this reason to keep the toilet seat down. The bathroom in short represents a place where money goes down the drain. Ponds and fountains stimulate Qi flow so if you have enough outdoor space it's advantageous to create one in a wealth direction.

Wood is an element born out of both Yin and Yang energy. It is the joining of the two energies that create plants and trees. Wood areas are also associated with wealth and prosperity. For wealth, health and general well-being you want to place wood elements like plants in these corresponding areas of your living environment. Wood also boosts your wealth when used in gardens and yards.

As far as color goes each element as was previously stated has corresponding colors. The South or Fire element direction is good for your recognition and fame. So using the corresponding colors of reds, oranges, purples and pinks in the recognition and fame areas can increase those aspects in your home or office. This is particularly good for your Career Qi flow if your career depends on those things. Colors also associated with the fire element are purples and pinks. You would not use black or blue in a Fire area to do so would be like putting out your own Fire so to speak. The reason is because black and blue are Water element colors and water puts a fire out.

The color green in your home when used in the East is excellent for improving health and family life. Blue is good in a North area to help with your career plans or in the East for health and family too. If blue is used in a South East direction it helps nurture the Wood element and increases prosperity and abundance.

Yellow in a South direction brings happiness and good times. White in a Western Area increases your creativity.

We can summarize each element as follows:

Fire – Red – South = Fame and Reputation

Lights, candles, paintings or artwork incorporating the color red, objects like red sofa pillows, a rug with the color red, a chair, red glass objects. Fire and Red are Yang energy. Yang is energizing.

Earth – Earth Yellow/Ochre/Beige to Brown/Earth Tone Colors and Materials – Southwest/Northeast/Center = Education and Knowledge.

Terra-cotta items, ceramic bowls, porcelain items, plants placed in terra-cotta or ceramic containers.

Metal – Gold/Silver/Pewter – West/Northwest = Fosters, Creativity and Children

Metal candle holder, picture frames, metal decorations, dinner plates decorated with silver, gold or both. Metal items in your kitchen, metal watering cans or decorations in the West corner of your garden.

Water – North = Career

Aquarium, fountains, ponds and fountains.

When we start to understand the ideas behind Feng Shui and incorporate them into our homes we may start to see positive changes. Little things like changing a dark blue vase in a South position makes a difference in the energy you circulate in your home and in turn the energy you manifest as a result of your environment.

Chapter 5: The Feng Shui Kua Number

In order to use Feng Shui tools properly you need to know what is called your Kua Number First. It is the Kua number that determines what your best compass directions for your home are, called "Auspicious Directions". It also determines the ones which are not good for you called the "Inauspicious Directions." It is by using the best directions determined by the Kua number that enhances the flow of Qi in your space. The Kua number which is also called Gua (pronounced Gwa) as in Ba Gua (we will discuss later) enables you to get the 4 corners or directions of a room or area.

In order to calculate the Kua number you need to know the persons gender and their year of birth. Here are the steps to calculate your Kua number.

1. You take your birth year and add the last two digits of it (Both sexes add the last 2 digits for their birth year). For example: If your birth year was 1957 you add 5+7=12

2. You then take the resulting number and reduce it to a single digit. Example: 12 is broken into two separate digits that are added together. 12 = 1+2=3

You now have to take that number and do further calculations based on your gender. If you are a female and your single digit is for example 3 you add 5 to it and you get the final number of 8. 3+5=8

If your birth number was a 5 and you add to it 5 getting 10 then you further reduce the number to a single digit as in step 1 so in this case 5+5=10 =1+0=1 and the Kua female number in this case based on the birth year would be a 1. So to get the female Kua number you add 5 to the birth year number after reducing it to a single digit.

But: For a Male Kua Number
1. Step one is the same; so if the birth year is 1957 for a male you also add the last two digits together and then reduce to a single digit. ex. 5+7 =12, 1+2=3
2. Now this is where the step changes with a male you subtract the single birth year from the number 10. So, in this case 10-3=7. The male number in this case is 7.

Now the next step in Feng Shui with Kua numbers is; depending on the Kua number determines if you are an East or West person.

EAST Group Kua Numbers are:
Kua Number 1, Kua Number 3, Kua Number 4, Kua Number 9

WEST Group Kua Numbers are:
Kua Number 2, Kua Number 5, Kua Number 6, Kua Number 7, Kua Number 8.

*SOME FENG SHUI SCHOOLS DO NOT USE THE NUMBER 5 SO IN THAT CASE FEMALES REPLACE THE NUMBER 5 WITH KUA 8 AND MEN REPLACE 5 WITH KUA 2.

Now here is a chart to determine the auspicious and inauspicious directions based on ones Kua number.

Kua Number	Auspicious	Inauspicious
1	South East	West
2	North East	East
3	South	South West
4	North	North West
5 (male)	North East	East
5 (female)	South West	South
6	West	South East
7	North West	North
8	South West	South
9	East	North East

Now for more specific types of luck with your Kua Number here is a chart for that. To get the maximum benefit of Qi and luck it is recommended that you sit or sleep with your head pointing in your Shen Chi or success direction.

Kua Number	Success Shen Chi	Health Tien Yi	Relationships Nien Yen	Personal Development Fu Wei
1	SE	E	S	N
2	NE	W	NW	SW
3	S	N	SE	E
4	N	S	E	SE

5 (male)	NE	W	NW	SW
5 (female)	SW	NW	W	NE
6	W	NE	SW	NW
7	NW	SW	NE	W
8	SW	NW	W	NE
9	E	SE	N	S

This is a chart of inauspicious specific directions. You do not want to sit or sleep in or facing this area at all if can be avoided. If you have to sit or sleep that way; it should be for the shortest period of time possible. Inauspicious directions cause problems in your life.

Kua Number	Unlucky Ho Hai	Five Ghosts Wu Kwei	Six Killing Lui Sha	Total loss Cheuh Ming
1	W	NE	NW	SW
2	E	SE	S	N
3	SW	NW	NE	W
4	NW	SW	W	NE
5 (male)	E	SE	S	N
5 (female)	S	N	E	SE
6	SE	E	N	S
7	N	S	SE	E
8	S	N	E	SE
9	NE	W	SW	NW

Chapter 6: Defining Your "Ba Gua"

A main tool used in Feng Shui is Ba Gua or BaGua. The Ba Gua is an octagon shaped grid that contains symbols from the I Ching oracle. Each section of the octagon has an I Ching symbol relevant to a compass direction. Ba Gua helps you to correlate and understand the various areas and spaces in and around your home and how they relate to your life. It is used to analyze the Qi of specific areas in your home. In literal translation Ba means 8 and Gua means triagram. Together the two make up the word 8 areas. So the BaGua is a grid, map or chart of the 8 directions and what they represent.

In order to define your "Ba Gua" you need to use a compass. The traditional Feng Shui compass is called a Lo Pan or you can use western compass as well (The main difference is the Lo Pan uses South as a Western compass points North). Each one of the 8 areas on the Ba Gua Grid has its own direction, element, color and area of life associated with it.

The 8 areas have also I Ching names and meanings. Each area is called Gua. Each Gua has a specific I Ching Symbol called Yao. Each Yao is a diagram of Yin and Yang energy and how they interact. The two short lines or hyphens are feminine or Yin and the solid line is Yang or male. The Yin lines correspond to the number Zero 0 and the Yang line to the number one 1.

Here is a description of each of the BaGua areas in terms of the I Ching Symbols or Yao.

Kun

The area farthest in the upper right corner means Earth. It represents the extreme female, mother. Mother represents the source/origin of life. The direction is south west and element is earth.

Zhen/Jen

The area left in the middle of the Yao Hsun and Ken. Zhen means thunder. Its direction is East and represents Health and Family. The element is Wood

Li

Li is the top most Yao. It means Fire. Li is the South Direction. It represents Fame and Reputation. It is also referred to as the illumination area because fame and our reputations can illuminate us. The element for this area is Fire.

Dui

The middle right area between Yao Kun and Chien is Dui. It represents Children and Creativity and its direction is West. It is this area that can also give us joy, imagination and even romance. The element for this area is Metal.

Ken/Gen

This is located in the farthest lower left corner. Gen which means mountain represents Knowledge, Cultivation, Sills and Spirituality. Its direction is Northeast and element is earth.

Kan

This is Kan which means Water. Its direction is the exact opposite of Li which is north. This area represents Career and its element is Water. Interesting enough the meeting of fire and water is considered the climax mating we refer to as orgasm. You have a peak and then decline.

Xun

The word Xun means the wind. This area is favored for Wealth and Prosperity. The direction is Southeast and element is Wood.

Qian/Chien

This is the Gua where the transformation of Yin to Yang is complete. It is the strongest of the Yang and total opposite of Kun. It is located in the farthest lower right corner of the chart or map. It represents the king, the father, the emperor, the boss and the Alpha male. This direction is northwest and represents helpful people and travel. The element is Metal.

The Lo Pan or Chinese Compass

Now that brings us to the LoPan or Compass that is used in Feng Shui. Lo means "Everything" Pan Means "Bowl" together they are interpreted to mean a tool that can access the mysteries of the universe. The Lo Pan or Feng Shui compass is a metal compass that has concentric directional formulas in rings around a magnetic needle. In most compasses the metal part sits on a wooden base representing earth. The base is also traditionally red. In Chinese culture red is both auspicious and protective. In this case it keeps the energy around the compass and the calculations clear.

What is different about the Feng Shui Lo Pan is it doesn't point north as its starting position like with Western Compasses. The Chinese Compass points South as its starting point 0. Interesting enough is the literal translation for the word of the needle that does the pointing in the Lo Pan is "Needle that points south".

There are three basic types of Feng Shui compasses from three different Chinese Feng Shui Schools. They are the San He, the San Yuan or Three Cycles School and the Flying Star which is the system derived from the Three Cycle School. The Chong He compasses includes formulas from both the San He and San Yuan schools. All three compasses have some formula rings in common. They include the 24 mountains, early and later heaven arrangements. Some Feng Shui masters actually make their own compasses. A professional Feng Shui compass can have over 40 rings of information on it.

In ancient times the Lo Pan was made out of tiger bones and hand painted. Today you can buy a Lo Pan in Asian Feng Shui Markets like the ones in New York City China Town or even on line. Not all the Feng Shui compasses are accurate you have to know which one to buy. And, you do not have to have a professional Feng Shui Master to use a Feng Shui compass. You need an accurate compass to do Feng Shui. That's what counts. Here is a diagram of a typical Feng Shui Compass:

Anyone who wishes to practice Feng Shui should familiarize themselves with the 24 mountains. The 24 mountains are the 24 sub directions featured in virtually every Feng Shui compass formula. These formulas are condensed on the Lo Pan into one ring around the whole compass. Each of the 24 mountains are divided into 15 degree segments. If you were to multiply the 15 X 24 you will have 360 degrees which is the circumference of the compass circle.

The sub directions are based on the Eight Mansions and Flying Star.

The Eight Mansions are 8 different Gua numbers which are calculated to find your Kua number. The system is commonly referred to as Ba Zhai or Eight Mansions. With Eight Mansions Qi flow is analyzed through cycles. Flying Star is a term used in the San Yuan School to define the flow of lucky Qi. The Eight Mansions and Flying Star are also the basis of the Water Dragon formulas and other sub formulas derived from the main Flying Star formula. The reason the compass is useful when doing Feng Shui although not mandatory for non-professionals is because Feng Shui characterizes buildings according to the direction they face upon being built. You can use a western compass to get the directions also. The western compass always find North as a starting point while the Lo Pan starts with South that's the only difference in terms of directions.

Here are the Specific Directions, Elements, Colors and Areas Associated with each of the Feng Shui Ba Gua locations according to compass directions.

*In Feng Shui remember that the 0 degree is the South Direction.

North (compass reading from 337.5 to 22.5)
Feng Shui Element: Water
Colors: and Blue and Black
Life Area: Career and Life Path / Fame

Northeast (compass reading from 22.5 to 67.5)
Feng Shui Element: Earth
Colors: Beige, Light Yellow, and Sandy/Earthy
Life Area: Spiritual Growth and Self Cultivation

East (compass reading from 67.5 to 112.5)
Feng Shui Element: Wood
Colors: Brown and Green
Life Area: Health and Family

Southeast (compass reading from 112.5 to 157.5)
Feng Shui Element: Wood
Colors: Brown and Green
Life Area: Money and Abundance

South (compass reading from 157.5 to 202.5)
Feng Shui Element: Fire
Colors: Red, Orange, Purple, Pink and Bright Yellow
Life Area: Fame & Reputation (a better translation is *the Light Within You*)

Southwest (compass reading from 202.5 to 247.5)
Feng Shui Element: Earth
Colors: Beige, Light Yellow, and Sandy/Earthy
Life Area: Love and Marriage

West (compass reading from 247.5 to 292.5)
Feng Shui Element: Metal
Colors: White and Grey
Life Area: Creativity and Children

FENG SHUI GUIDE

The BaGua

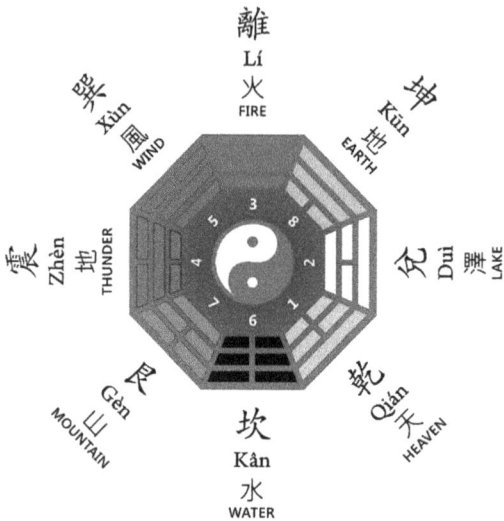

In Feng Shui you would use the Ba Gua Grid/Chart or Map with your Kua number which determines your best directions on the compass. The Ba Gua determines the spaces in your area. It has 8 spaces and the Ba Gua is either in squares or an octagon shape. Each of the spaces corresponds to an aspect of life. Using the grid as a guide you assess each living space in corresponding aspects to the grid.

Life situation areas on the Feng Shui Bagua Map:

1 *Career, Life's Purpose*
2 *Relationship, Partnership*
3 *Family, Community*
4 *Wealth, Prosperity*
5 *Health, Life Force*
6 *Helpful People, Travel*
7 *Creativity, Children*
8 *Knowledge, Wisdom*
9 *Fame, Reputation*

This is the Ba Gua Map for Eastern Feng Shui

This map is used for your home or business as a whole.

Wealth and Prosperity Location: SE corner Colors: Purples, Reds and Greens	Fame and Reputation Location: South corner Colors: Reds and Oranges	Love and Marriage Location: SW corner Colors: Reds, Pinks and Whites
Health and Family Location: East corner Colors: Blues and Greens	Earth YOU Location: Center Colors: Yellows and Earth tones	Creativity and Children Location: West Corner Colors: Metals, White and Pastels
Knowledge and Self Cultivation Location: NE Corner Colors: Black, Blues and Greens	Career Location: North corner Colors: Black and Dark Blues	Helpful People and Travel Location: NW Corner Colors: White, Grey and Black

The Elements:
- South-Fire
- East-Wood
- North-Water
- West-Metal
- Center-Earth

This is the Ba Gua Map for Western Feng Shui

This map is based on individual rooms of home or business.

FENG SHUI GUIDE

Wealth and Prosperity Location: Rear Left Colors: Purples, Reds and Greens	Fame and Reputation Location: Rear Middle Colors: Reds and Oranges	Love and Marriage Location: Rear Right Colors: Reds, Pinks and White
Health and Family Location: Middle Left Colors: Blues and Greens	Earth YOU Location: Center Colors: Yellows and Earth Tones	Creativity and Children Location: Middle Right Colors: Pastels and White
Knowledge and Cultivation Location: Front Left Colors: Blacks and Blues	Career Location: Front Middle Colors: Black and Dark Blues	Helpful People and Travel Location: Front Right Colors: White, Grey and Black

Entrance

Entrance to your individual rooms or offices will be in one of the three front areas of Knowledge and Cultivation, Career, or Helpful People and Travel.

Elements
- Family and Reputation: Fire
- Health and Family: Wood
- Career: Water
- Creativity and Children: Metal
- Center(YOU):Earth

Chapter 7: Finding the Missing Ba Gua Areas in Your Residence

We all do not have apartments and homes that match all the parts of the BaGua Map. When this is the case we say that the BaGua is incomplete and the energy is weak. In most cases it's not that the areas are missing it's just that they are smaller in comparison to others. When areas are small or missing it is considered in Feng Shui to be out of balance or negative. This is said to create an energy void or weak spot in the BaGua of a home. These areas are called BaGua void areas, BaGua negative areas and BaGua weak areas. An example of a missing BaGua area would be like you don't have the "Career Area" BaGua in your home according to the Ba Gua Map. In this case you would need to do remedies to strengthen the Career area weakness.

If you do find that your home is lacking in one or more BaGua area; you need to do things to help compensate for that weak energy. The idea is when the energy is corrected it is referred to in Feng Shui as cures. Cures help the energy flow and balance the area that is lacking. The center of the BaGua which is also the heart cannot be missing. When you understand the five elements and directions you can use simple cures like mirrors, colors, fountains etc. to increase the Qi in the weak or lacing area.

Tips for the Missing BaGua Locations

Missing North BaGua - The BaGua area associated with the north is Career. So you want the remedies to reflect your intent on career. Since the element for the north is water most remedies or cures for this missing Direction would either be water or nurturing elements such as metal.

Things that help for a weak North location are big round or oval mirrors, pictures and art in black and white to reflect those people or things in your career that you admire. Any kind of actual water like a fountain is good in this area. The placement of tall lights are considered a good tool for expansion. Wall murals with deep blues of the sky as are colors of the sea (blues) are positive in this direction. Pictures of water, art reflecting water also works in this area. You can also actually paint the walls in the missing or weak North BaGua area blue.

The animal that symbolizes the North is the Black Turtle. The turtle represents longevity, endurance and strength. In Feng Shui the black turtle symbolizes hills behind a dwelling. The hills signify support and offer the location protection and support. In most conventionally designed homes the front door faces south and the back faces North.(Remember in Feng Shui Our North is their South). In this case the black turtle represents the back of a building or dwelling.

Missing Northeast BaGua - The element used for cures if the Northeastern BaGua is missing is Earth element remedies or of the Fire element which nourishes Earth. This area is associated with spirituality and personal growth. It is also the place for the location of the divine presence your life. The cures for this area should reflect thing to energize your personal growth as well as things that enhance the reflection of your spirituality.

In a weak Northeast BaGua you want art that reflects the Earth element. Pictures of mountains are very auspicious for this. However the art you use needs to be open in the picture. What is meant by open is you don't want a picture of one mountain with no spaces around it. This includes one that enclosed between other things because this can further block the energy flow. A mountain with land on both sides that spreads out is ideal. This is particularly true for missing Northeast areas.

You also want to pick things that reflect your deeper self as well as reflections of your spirituality to go in this area. You do need to be mindful that Water or Metal element objects should be avoided in this area. Art with Fire elements is very positive in this area. Things like candles, especially tall ones in reds, oranges and purples do well in this area. You also want to use earth shapes (squares) avoid water and metal element shapes and colors in this area as well. Tall lights work in this area too. You can also paint the walls earth or fire colors. Fire colors are reds, purples, oranges, pinks and strong yellows. Earth colors are yellows, beiges those colors considered as earth tones.

Missing East BaGua - The element for the East is Wood. So, your cures need the Wood element or Water element which nourishes and strengthens Wood. This BaGua area is associated with Life and Family. It is very important that in this area you try and maximize Qi flow to optimize health on all levels. Health in this case is defined as physical, mental, emotional and spiritual. Included in health are aspects of harmonious energy to maintain peace in the family.

Since this is a Wood element area you want to incorporate Wood art furniture and even plants. Art or pictures depicting health and family harmony are for this area. Strong Fire and Metal elements should be avoided in this area. Use Water element objects and art work in this area. They serve as a visual pathway to open the area. Fountains or other water décor in black and blue as well as wood décor in browns and greens are right for this area. You can paint the walls browns and greens in this area to open the energy as well as using tall lights. Mirrors in this area can work too. Ideal mirrors for this direction are square and rectangular shaped with wooden frames.

In Feng Shui the green dragon is the celestial animal representing the east. It signifies the left side of the house looking towards the front door. For the inside of the home the green dragon signifies protection for those who live there. Hills that represent the green dragon are higher than those of the white tiger behind the home. The green dragon is Yang energy. He symbolizes strength, goodness, courage and endurance. He is anything symbolizing vigilance and security. The white tiger of the west is inseparable with the green dragon.

Missing Southeast BaGua - This area is related to Prosperity and Abundance. The element related to this BaGua is Wood and is nurtured by Water. So this area needs Wood elements and Water reinforcements when it is missing or weak. It is recommended to express prosperity and all its forms in this directional area. This means both the material wealth and the blessings life has to offer you as well.

As with all missing BaGua areas you have to compensate the area with appropriate elemental objects to reinforce the energy and increase the flow of Qi. In addition to Wood element objects and furniture you want to have things that express abundance. Photo graphs and pictures depicting what wealth means to you is ideal. Do avoid those shapes and colors that deal with too much Fire or Metal in this area. Any water elements should be clear and moving in this area like a water fall or fountain. The shapes should be square or rectangular objects for wood in this area and wavy and flowing for water. The colors for this area are greens, browns blues and black. Plants are a great Feng Shui Cure for this area too. You can paint the walls any of the Wood and Water element colors. But also a small amount of purple and red can be added in wealth areas to stimulate activation. But these two colors need to be in very small amounts. Mirrors that are Square or Rectangle with wooden frames are good accents for this area also.

Missing South BaGua - The South is governed by the element Fire and Wood which nourishes the Fire element. To fortify the weak and missing area of Fame and Reputation you have to use Fire and Wood elements. The literal translation for this BaGua area "is the light within". In this area you want to use elements that show what you want to be known for, what light do you bring to the world, what is the essence of your fame and reputation. You want art and other things that really speak to your heart about what you want to be known for and as.

You want to use Fire and Wood elemental objects in this area. Candles in fire colors and wooden décor is ideal for this area. The colors you want to use in this area are reds, pinks, purples, oranges and strong yellows for the Fire and greens and browns for the wood. You want to use triangular shapes for the fire element and squares and rectangles for the wood. Tall lights are good for the cure in this area. Lights are a form of fire. You want to avoid Water elements in a Southern area. A fireplace is a very good cure for a Southern BaGua especially if it is missing or incomplete. You can also paint the walls in any of the fire or wood colors.

The red Phoenix is the animal of this direction. Red Phoenix protects the front of a home. It is the front door where energy enters the home. In landscape terms a low hill found in low ground in surrounding front areas to the home is auspicious. This landscape position represents the foot stool which signifies luxury and an ease in one's life. In Chinese mythology the body of the Phoenix represents the five human qualities. The head is virtue, the wings are duty, the back is ritually correct behavior, breast is humanity and the stomach reliability.

Missing West BaGua - This is the area of Children and Creativity. The elements that need nurturing in a weak or missing West BaGua are Metal and its nurturing element is Earth. In this area it's important to have objects and things reflecting your creative endeavors as well as support for the energy of your children. Use art and objects made from the metal element as well as the earth element here. You want things in this area to reinforce and strengthen free flowing creative thought and energy. Avoid Fire and Water elements in this area. This is a good area to put photographs of your children. Also art and objects that evoke happiness and joyful moments. Any artwork that your children have created is a good energy booster in this area.

Tall lighting is a plus in this area. The colors are shades of grey, white and earth colors which are yellows, beige's and earth tones. The shapes that compliment this area are Round and Oval for metal and square and rectangular for earth. Fire and Water elements including colors and shapes should be avoided in this area. Of course you can paint the walls in Metal and Earth colors in this area.

The white tiger is the animal that protects and guides this direction. The white tiger represents land to the right of where you are looking. It could be a building or a hill. White tiger is Yin, passive and feminine. Where ever White Tiger is the Dragon co-exists. The two are inseparable. If there is a position for White Tiger there is always one for Dragon even if it isn't obvious and vice versa. The white tiger symbolizes strength. One of the stories is that White Tiger and Dragon mated and created an abundance of Qi because of their vast cosmic force in the universe. Tiger is also one of the best protections against evil intention of strangers.

Missing Northwest BaGua - This is the BaGua of Helpful People/Blessings and Travel. The elements for this area are Metal and Earth. For this area you want to include objects that reflect things to attract beneficial people in your life. It is equally important to express your gratitude in this area through your object choices for the helpful and beneficial energy you already receive in your life. You want to avoid Fire and Water elemental things, colors and shapes in this area. This area is good for things like pictures of people who have benefited you in your life and also travel pictures. Also, places you would like to go to are in the right place here. Tall lights and tall sculptures are good in this area. Also round objects for Metal and Square for earth is the way to go in this area. White and greys of different shades are the colors you want to use in this area. So are earth tones, yellows and beiges. Again you want to avoid Fire and Water elemental things including colors and shapes in this area. Painting the walls in earth and metal colors works here too.

Chapter 8: How to Utilize Ba Gua Areas

For each of the areas on the BaGua Grid/Map there are tips to make them auspicious for you. You want to use each area to the utmost that its energy is generated to full capacity. By maximizing the energy of a particular BaGua you enhance that area of your life. Feng Shui increases the flow of positive energy in your home or office. All of the spaces should be neat and orderly. Clutter blocks the flow of Qi. With that in mind there is a brief overview of how to utilize each of the BaGua Areas for optimum Qi.

Wealth and Prosperity BaGua Area

This is the Southeast corner of your home or business. In an individual room it is located in the rear left section of the BaGua. Wealth takes on many forms in addition to money. You use this area to increase your finances, to increase raising your funds for a specific item (ex: a new car) or if you just want more abundance in your life. Abundance can mean more friends, love, fun, whatever you consider abundance for you. Keeping this in mind you want to consider what you want and what you want to use to symbolize your desires.

Tips to Enhance this BaGua Area:

Enhancing Colors: Reds, Purples and Greens

1. Tying three Chinese coins with a red ribbon and hang or place them in this corner is auspicious. If you do so make sure the coins are in increments of 3, 6 or 8. 8 is the most auspicious powerful money manifestation number
2. Where you work in this area hang a chime from the ceiling, chimes in this area promote good wisdom and good Qi.
3. Water features like a water fountain keep money flowing but put it in a corner in this area conducive to water. If you can't put a water fountain then use a picture of flowing water.
4. A fish tank or bowl in the wealth corner promotes financial growth. As your fish grow so does your money from that corner.
5. If you have a back yard and it slopes downward in the south eastern corner away from the house then put a light fixture there. Shine it upward towards the house a couple of hours a day. You are symbolically directing money towards your home.
6. Place a windmill, weather vane, a pin wheel, whirly wig or any spinning thing in the far left corner of your back yard. This stimulates the movement of air and Qi. This also attracts wealth.
7. Slow growing plants represent slow growing wealth, particularly jade plants.
8. The far left corner of any room is a wealth area. So Place 3 plants together with round leaves in those areas of your rooms. Round leaf plants look like coins. If they bare red or purple flowers even better.

9. Plug all drains in the home up when not using them. This symbolizes the idea of preventing money from going down the drain.
10. Keep the toilet seat down when not in use. This reinforces the idea of not letting money go down the toilet.
11. Use earth tones in rooms that have an abundance of water like bathrooms and kitchens. The color is like a damn to keep your money longer.
12. Keep you stove clean and in optimum condition. The Chinese feel food is connected to wealth.
13. Hang or place a mirror above or behind the stove so it reflects twice as many burners as before. Be careful with this one.
14. Put pictures of things you want to buy in the south eastern corner. This will charge it.
15. Make sure your doors open completely in your home so as not to limit your possibilities of wealth and living in comfort and ease.
16. Place 3 similar objects in either the wealth area of your living room or bed room. The traditional colors of wealth are gold, purple, reds and greens. However you can use colors that express wealth to you. You can do things like three similar pictures, three brass candle holders with red candles or even 3 red bowls filled with coins.
17. Hang around faceted clear crystal on an 18 inch red cord in your living room in the rear wealth corner. The red cord is an activator and the crystal swinging gives the energy in the corner a boost. Hang near a window and get a rainbow which is an added health boost.
18. Keep valuables, coin collections, piggy banks, safes, jewelry and things you value in your far left corner in your bedroom. This amplifies the wealth you accrue there. If you cannot store your valuables there then put things that represent wealth to you there.

Fame and Reputation BaGua Area

This location is at the Southern corner of your home or business. In individual rooms it is located in the rear middle BaGua area. Fame isn't limited to career only. What we do to earn a living doesn't necessarily mean what we want to do with our lives as a career. Nor is it a means to define who we are. A person can work as a cashier and have aspirations of being a great singer. So in this area you would put things that reflect aspirations of what you want to become not necessarily the job you currently hold. This is the area to express those things that you want to be viewed as in terms of your reputation, or what you wish to be known in others eyes for. In this corner it is important that you express who you want to be and not what others want you to be.

Tips to Enhance this BaGua Area:

Enhancing Colors: Reds and Oranges

1. The color red is key for the fame and reputation area. You can use red for everyday objects in a room with this area as well as in the Southern corner or rear middle area of your home. Red activates the fame and reputation energy needed to succeed in your goals. Soft furnishing like upholstery, lampshades, drapes, bedspreads and rugs work great in this area.
2. Fire element objects work good in this area too. Things like fire places in this BaGua Area energize it with positive Qi. If there is no room for a fire place things like candles and incense are auspicious in this area too.
3. Hanging a panting with red as the dominant color is a good energy booster as is using a wooden frame or any wood element because wood nourishes fire.
4. It is very good Qi energy to display things of merit that you achieved like diplomas, awards, trophies, letters of recognition or any other symbols of successes.

5. This area should have lots of lights. Use bright lights in this BaGua; twinkling lights, spot lights or chandeliers.
6. Display something in this area that you would like to be known for. It can be a model or a photograph either is sufficient to help promote positive Qi in this area.
7. Put up or place physical reminders of your goals like charts and visuals in this area to help focus the Qi for this BaGua.
8. Also display work of humanitarian and unselfish nature here. For example a letter of recognition for your work with abused children and things of that nature. Helping others promotes good Qi.

Love and Marriage BaGua Area

The Love and Relationships/Marriage area is located at the South Western corner of your home or business. In an individual room it is the right rear section of the BaGua. This is the area of Love. Love reigns here. You can attract new love or enhance your current love in this area.

Tips to Enhance this BaGua Area:

Enhancing Colors: Reds, Pinks and Whites

1. Hang pictures of you and your mate in this area
2. Place a pair of objects in this corner, one representing you and one representing your mate like a pair of mandarin ducks or a pair of cranes who mate for life. This represents successful partnering. Place them in the rear far right corner or the southwest corner of the bedroom.
3. Mandarin Ducks are a symbol of lovers and marital bliss. It creates the Qi for tying the knot. Placing a pair of ducks in the South Western corner of your home; or in the far right corner of your living room or bed room which activates the love and marriage Qi.

4. Remove or Cover Mirrors in the bedroom. A mirror facing the bed from any side (this means ceilings, wall, closet door or dressing table) reflects the couple in bed. This can also create a failure in the marriage or relationship due to third party interference or infidelities.
5. Televisions are considered like mirrors and should not be in the bed room.
6. Place the bed where it is not in direct line with the door. Especially do not have your feet facing the door. They take the dead from the bedroom feet first.
7. Do not place the bed under a window.
8. Your bed should be accessible from three sides if you want to attract or keep a partner.
9. Sleep with your head in one of the auspicious directions particularly the Sheng Chi direction.
10. Treat yourself to fresh flowers and replace them often. However do not place them in the Southwest corner or the right rear corner of any room. Flowers clash with the element of Romance which is earth.
11. Remove all sad, abstract, dark or scary artwork from your bedroom. Bedrooms should be peaceful, safe and a fantasy room. Bedrooms are for sleeping and making love. Any art objects like swords, guns, sad or dark things encourage anger, and fighting as well as negative dreams.
12. Buy a gift that symbolizes a new relationship. Place it in a prominent space in your home so every time you pass it you can see yourself meeting your perfect mate.
13. Hang a painting of Peonies in the living room on the south wall for love.
14. Remove any objects that remind you of work from the bedroom as well as pictures of family and friends from master bed rooms.
15. Do not keep things under the bed it can cause detrimental arguments.

16. Place two red candles in the southwest corner or your space or far right corner of your bedroom. Light them every night for a few minute to invoke love.
17. Use beads and fabrics as an alternative to doors. This enhances or visual senses as well as the sense of touch.
18. Hanging heart shaped pink crystals in sunny windows catches sunlight which creates rainbows and in turn brings good Yang energy which is love Qi.
19. A wind chime in a sunny window also produces good Yang Qi.
20. Plant 2 things like two trees that bear fruit in the right hand corner of your back yard. It symbolizes a fruitful relationship.
21. If you cannot plant 2 things in that space for whatever reason a table with two chairs in that corner is good also. Place fresh flowers on that table.
22. Include the colors of romance in your bedroom. That means shades of pinks, reds and white. A red bedspread isn't recommended because it can ignite anger (red can cause anger as well as passion.) Remember a little red goes a long way in the bedroom.
23. Place 2 red hearts in one of your relationship areas. This will help your present relationship or if you are single help you find a new exciting one.
24. If you are single make two wish lists. One list will have the qualities of an ideal mate for you and the other the qualities of an ideal relationship that you want. These are two separate things. Be very specific about what you want. Whatever you want write in on the list. Do not use negative statements like for instance I don't want a man who cheats. Instead say I want a man who is monogamous. Spend at least 10 minutes a day with the lists. Get all your senses involved. Make copies of the lists and put them where you can see them. Every time you pass the lists see yourself meeting your ideal mate. Before you know it you will.

25. If your bathtub is in the far right of the bathroom place two items that are of course water proof there representing you and your mate. It can be two rubber ducks, shampoo and conditioner or two pink rose quartz crystals.
26. Relocate any exercise equipment to another location. It makes for the idea that you have to work hard for your relationship; or hard to have a good one.
27. To represent your relationship or a relationship in the kitchen use things like 2 red canisters, a vase on the table with 2 red or pink flowers in it. You can also have red or pink salt and pepper shakers or 2 red or pink flower producing plants in this area.
28. If you are single set your table for two and visualize your mate there with you at dinner. You can even light to dinner candles.
29. The double happiness symbol is auspicious in relation to activating marriage luck. If you are already married it enhances the marriage by adding eternal and wonderful Qi to the marriage. You can paint the symbol on a rock in red and place it in a southwest corner of your home.

Health And Family BaGua Area

This BaGua is located in the East Corner of your home or Business. In individual rooms this BaGua is located in the middle left section of the BaGua. This is the BaGua of New beginnings, health issues (both physical and mental), family and friends who are like family.

Tips to Enhance this BaGua Area:

Enhancing Colors: Blues and Greens

1. Hang pictures of family and friends in this area. If there are three people in a particular picture make sure they are staggered. 3 people in a line side by side is bad Feng Shui.
2. Books on herbs and healing are great to put in this corner.
3. Hanging or placing crystals in this corner are very good Qi boosters.

FENG SHUI GUIDE

4. Clear crystals give the room a rainbow which is very good Qi health therapy. Rose crystals are good for emotional Qi. Green Crystals are good for physical health Qi. Blue crystals promote mental clarity. Red Crystals activate all the energies in whatever space needs activating. Remember a little red goes a long way.
5. Putting blue and green items in this corner help positive Qi flow.
6. Things made of wood nurture this area. Wooden picture frames are good.
7. Mirrors in this area are good cures for bad and sudden illnesses.
8. Things in this area to remind you of family and close friends are good in this area.
9. This is the perfect area for exercise equipment
10. If you don't have a pet get one. They stimulate life force energy because that is what they have. They represent unconditional love.
11. This is a good place to put art and furniture that is inherited from loved ones.
12. Objects that are rectangular and columns work great for Qi in this area because of its elements.
13. Hang or put a reminder of fun you had in this physical world (can be a souvenir , a sport object like a ball, etc.)
14. Hang things from your favorite sports team in this area.
15. Help a neighbor clean their yard it spreads good Qi.
16. Make sure there are no over beams over items like beds, desks, couches, because these items are like cutting into you energies
17. Do not keep electric blankets on when you are sleeping they can affect your Qi flow.
18. Burn incense, oils, scented candles, etc. Good smells have a positive effect on us and the environment we live in.
19. Buy yourself a gift representing optimum health and put it where you can see it.
20. Wear green. It's the color of health and healing.

21. If any of your views are unpleasant from your windows place a mirror across to send it back outside.
22. Clear Clutter outside the house and inside. Clutter blocks positive Qi flow and creates negativity.
23. Wear pink colors to melt anger. Wearing and using green also promotes soul soothing and restoration
24. Place items that represent longevity in the health area like cranes, tortoises any animal or plant that lives a long time.
25. For those who have trouble conceiving; place a Dragon in this area.

The Center BaGua - You/The Earth

The Center of the BaGua is called the You or Earth Area. In your home or business it is located in the center, in individual rooms it's the center of the room. This area represents you in relation to the planet. Until we are clear of what we want and who we are; the universe can do little to assist us. As we grow we go through different experiences that affect who we are and our beliefs causing us to change. The constant changes can confuse the universe so you have to stand firm in who you are and what you want.

Tips to Enhance this BaGua Area:

Enhancing Colors: Yellows and Earth tones

1. Take the time to ask yourself what you really want. Listen to your soul answer and write it down as you hear it.
2. View any changes in your life as adventures not disruptions. We have go through changes. It is part of life.
3. Mediate to learn who you really are
4. Yoga is another good way to learn your inner self and receive benefits from knowing your inner being
5. Keep your focus and attention on your intentions
6. Dream big and let no person or thing stand in your way
7. Dance; it enhances who you are

8. Listen to music it feeds the soul
9. Rejoice in who you are; a child of God
10. It's time to let go of the old, get out of your comfort zone, that's what Feng Shui is about changing energy.
11. Never give up on yourself.

Creativity And Children BaGua Area

This area is located in the West corner of your Business or Home. In individual rooms this area is the middle right location of the BaGua. This area is about creativity and its inception. This is the area for conceiving ideas, children and plans. You name it, conceiving and creativity are nurtured in this area. This is the BaGua if you want to be more creative and improve relationships with children as well.

Tips to Enhance this BaGua Area:

Enhancing Colors: Metals, Pastels and Whites

1. This is the perfect area for arts and crafts, hobbies and creative endeavors.
2. TV's Stereos and Computers are best in this area
3. Photos of family and friends are good here too
4. Sentimental things and mementos you have kept from your childhood are very good here.
5. Use fresh flowers here, try to keep in the white and pastel colors to release the positive Qi because of the colors of this BaGua Area.
6. A piece of artwork from an artist you admire
7. This is the area to put up or keep things to remind you of your goals such as pictures, brochures anything related to your goal
8. The same goes for your dreams, here is the place to put the symbols for your dreams
9. Statues and Figurines of your desires are good in this area too.
10. If you want a baby, place baby things in this area. Even things like birth announcements are good in this area if you want a

child.
11. If your baby days are over put things made by you for you in this corner representing your creativity.
12. This is a good area for a kids room
13. If you have pets keep their things in this area

Knowledge And Self Cultivation BaGua Area

This BaGua area is located in the Northeastern corner of your home or business. In an individual room this area is located in the front left of the BaGua map. This area represents our desires to know more, to become more in our lives and to learn more. This BaGua is about self-expansion and growing.

Tips to Enhance this BaGua Area:

Enhancing Colors: Blues, Greens and Blacks

1. A book case in this area reflecting your interests and your knowledge, its good if the book shelf has a door on it but if it doesn't bring the books to the front of the shelf.
2. A globe in this area enhances your knowledge of the world
3. Things related to writing: writing tables, pens and pencils are good in this area
4. The color red activates educational success. Place some red in the Southeastern section of this area for that purpose. Remember a little red only because red goes a long way.
5. This corner benefits from things like pots, urns and other containers made from clay
6. Pictures reflecting your inner strength like posters of mountains are good in this area.
7. A nice comfortable chair in this area for thinking and reading.
8. Good lighting is a must in this area
9. Wind chimes increase the Qi for knowledge but in this area they are not to be made from metal
10. Plants represent growth put some in this area.

11. Items expressing growth, could be anything like tape measures, encyclopedias or any type of educational book
12. Keep this area clutter free or it creates clutter in your life
13. Reading more enhances this area
14. Hang a Carp windsock in this area to generate the ease with which knowledge is obtained and flows

Career BaGua Area

The BaGua area that promotes career is located in the North corner of your home or business. In an individual room this BaGua area is located in the front middle section of a room or office. Career reigns in this BaGua area, so just because you may currently wait tables does not mean that that is your career or aspirations of a career.

Tips to Enhance this BaGua Area:

Enhancing Colors: Blues and Blacks

1. Hanging chimes outside your front door is good Qi for a promotion or more career opportunities
2. Hang a Brightly colored flag , windsock or banner in your front yard.
3. Place a bird bath or feeder in your yard, attracting wild life attracts positive energy to your home
4. Terrapins are believed to bring fantastic luck into their owners lives. So place a picture of one on the North Wall of your Career BaGua or actually get one or a tortoise to keep in this area.
5. Write down what you would like to do if money was not an issue for a career. Keep several of them and place them about. Ask for divine assistance and remember to be grateful.
6. Make sure your address is clearly visible in the day and lit at night.
7. Clear clutter and plant debris and keep it clear in your yard. Clutter blocks the flow of opportunity

8. Place a colorful inviting welcome mat at the front door
9. Place a water fountain, water bubbles or fountain as an indicator that you are going in the right direction.
10. Spring clean even in the winter. Clutter limits the choices we have.
11. If you have stairs place a heavy object there at the base like a plant or statue. The reason for this is the energy going down the stairs is like a waterfall of energy so it's good to slow it down a little
12. Keep your doors opened because closed doors limit your opportunity energy
13. Try and not over power your rooms with too much furniture. Furniture can block the flow of Qi.
14. Try and keep bare walls to a minimum in your home the reason for this is bare walls make us feel like we have very little or no choices
15. Make sure all the clocks in your house are in working order, if not give them away or fix them. Otherwise time stands still or creates stagnation when clocks don't work.
16. Use a blue or black rug at the front door to stimulate the flow of opportunities like water coming in your home symbolically.
17. Make sure there are lots of colors around you where you are working. Color stimulates and rejuvenates mental ability
18. If possible place your desk to have a good view of the room and the front door. If you can place your desk in the far left which is the wealth corner even better.
19. Mirrors in this area serve to reflect your personal path
20. Use symbols in this area to reflect your personal career or chosen career path.
21. Print and frame the job description you want. Place it in this area to remind you of your chosen career path.
22. A green plant or plants in this area symbolizes career growth
23. A frames positive affirmation will remind you or your true path.

Helpful People And Travel BaGua Area

This BaGua are is located in the Northwestern corner of your home or business. In an individual room this area is located at the right front section of the BaGua. This BaGua area represents the Qi to bring helpful people to us and our lives or guides us to helpful people on a daily basis. This area also represents helpful beings like God, angels, spirit guides and spirit animals. This is also the area representing travel.

Tips to Enhance this BaGua Area:

Enhancing Colors: White, Greys and Black

1. Visualize how you want people to help you, especially when you are embarking on a particular endeavor
2. Use affirmations that coincide with your wishes and desires
3. This is the area for religious symbols of your belief system. Objects related to your religious belief system like statues are very good here too. This will bring helpful beings to assist you.
4. You can place objects and things of honor for your mentors here. Examples would be things like their, pictures, books, cards etc.
5. Hanging wind chimes in the Northwestern corner of your Career BaGua or office. This rules the quality of patron luck.
6. Never sit with your back to the door. If it can't be avoided then place a mirror above the desk to reflect the front door or on the desk facing the front door to reflect it to you. This prevents being stabbed in the back by enemies.
7. Place a ceramic statue of a fierce cat preferably a tiger(or lion, panther or leopard) outside your office door. Do not place it inside the office door unless you were born the year of the Tiger. This provides protection against people who are not helpful with interfering with your business matters.
8. Place brochures in this area for where you want to travel to

9. Find information about where you would like to travel and put it around this area so you can view it frequently.
10. Visualize you already at the destination you want to travel to and use positive affirmations to reaffirm your desires.
11. Make an itinerary of your trip and view it often
12. Replicas such as toys, models or pictures of vehicles of travel be it cars, boats or airplanes are good in this area.
13. Place statues and pictures of eagles soaring in this area will attract travel for you to new places. Beware not eagles in attack mode.
14. Place the trigram Chien or Qian in this area which represents heaven. To achieve this place three pictures in the same manner as Chien in the office area.

These tips are just the top of the iceberg in Feng Shui. Feng Shui is much deeper than just the advice found in this book but for a beginner these tips can prove very helpful and open up the world of Feng Shui to you to delve deeper into if you wish.

Chapter 9: The Art of Feng Shui

This book is literally an introduction to the science/art of Feng Shui. The information given is basic enough for anyone to use and understand the principles. Feng Shui can get very involved and complicated as you move on to master it. This is just a touch of what it is and even this bit can change someone's life for the better if they apply what is in this little book.

Feng Shui is considered a "Traditional Cure". It is used to manipulate energy according to its auspicious possibilities by directing the flow in particular directions and ridding negative energy the same way by dispersing it. The main thing is that the Qi in one's environment is flowing in a positive and harmonious direction and reinforced with elemental considerations based on the directional flow.

I would like at this time to just mention poison arrows which are sharp edges created by things in the home or environment that are directed towards you by their placement. It can be a wall edge pointing in the direction of your bed or even a table corner situated in a non-auspicious direction. These are just some of the many types of poison arrows that Feng Shui cures if you apply it based on understand the concept. The idea behind poison arrows are what is called Shar Qi which is also known as Killing Breath. Killing breath blocks and stagnates the flow of Qi thus killing its positive movement. This in turn becomes detrimental energy for the residents of a home that has Shar Qi.

Most Feng Shui cures are inexpensive but there have been cases where the Shar Qi is so severe that people have moved from the current home or office. The goal of Feng Shui is to remove all the poison arrows from a living or working environment.

Most homes with poison arrows can be treated with mirrors, crystals and rearranging the furniture. Changing the colors of things in certain areas does wonders too especially if it is not a Qi evoking color for a particular area.

The basic poison arrow is two walls meeting in a sharp angle that is pointed at you. It comes at you like a dart of an arrow across your bed, where you sit or in a location in the environment where you spend a lot of your time. The easiest cure for this kind of poison arrow is to hang a crystal from the ceiling directly in front of the corner in question. For an average size room a 30mm sized crystal will do the trick but if it's an extra-large room with tall ceilings then 40mm is the way to go. You can also use mirrors to deflect poison arrows or negative energy by placing it between you and the thing you want to deflect. The mirror should be at list 6 inches in size to be effective. You can use a mirror to deflect things like cemetery or funeral home views, noisy or trashy neighbors or whatever you view as negative.

The main thing is that Feng Shui is a vital tool when used properly can enhance our lives and that of our family. Good Feng Shui when using the BaGua properly even enhances other aspects of our life by generating positive energy around us. Everyone can benefit from positive energy. For those that really want their life Feng Shui fortified they hire professional Feng Shui masters. It is the Feng Shui master who analyzes the various aspects of your life and prescribes the appropriate cures based on their findings. If you want to learn yourself you can start with this book and then branch out to either study with a master or read more advanced material. There is so much information today that anyone can learn about and use Feng Shui to improve their lives from many sources and I hope this book inspires you to do so.

MEET THE AUTHOR

Spiritualist Kate Dunn invests her energy to help people find peace and rest. She utilizes Feng Shui to redesign her clients' rooms in order to give them the optimum emotional and mental experience of their space. Once the energy in their homes is positive, she comes alongside her clients as a spiritual advisor and healer.

Kate wasn't always known for her wisdom and peaceful energy. By the time she graduated college, she was a walking ball of stress. She was constantly chasing "success" and trying to please the people around her. Work was constantly on her mind, and every space in her home was an extension of her office. After a couple of years, she had received three promotions, made zero friends, and developed an ulcer. Something had to change.

It was actually her manicurist who suggested she enlist Marie, a spiritual advisor. It took Kate weeks to make the call, but eventually she figured there was nothing to lose. They met in her home, and immediately Marie recognized the lack of balance in her life. She reworked her space and together they reclaimed it as a space that would be full of life and rest. Once she detoxed from being a workaholic, Marie helped Kate to use natural alternative strategies to help her body to heal.

It's been ten years since Kate's radical transformation, but she's happy to report that she now actually enjoys her life! Taking the time to center herself and her energy has been wonderful, and it has left her with a deep sense of gratitude that she stepped up and fought for a more fulfilling life.

www.ingramcontent.com/pod-product-compliance
Ingram Content Group UK Ltd.
Pitfield, Milton Keynes, MK11 3LW, UK
UKHW022120230426
12048UKWH00010BA/627